MW01114332

BREAKING YOUR CURSES, RECEIVING YOUR BLESSINGS

J.D. & Ramona Duffield
P.O. Box 1327
Ashland VA, 23005

BY

RAMONA DUFFIELD

Fairmont Books is a ministry of The McDougal Foundation, Inc., a Maryland nonprofit corporation dedicated to spreading the Gospel of the Lord Jesus Christ to as many people as possible in the shortest time possible.

Published by:

𝓕airmont Books

P.O. Box 3595
Hagerstown, MD 21742-3595
www.mcdougalpublishing.com

ISBN 1-58158-067-3

Printed in the United States of America
For Worldwide Distribution

Dedication

To my wonderful Christian mother, Iola. I love her so much and I am very grateful for her. She prayed for me, loved me, and taught me to love and know God. I will forever be thankful for her grounding me in the Lord so that I would not be able to turn my back on God.

To my wonderful husband, J.D. He is my faithful companion, lover, greatest supporter, and best friend.

To my three precious daughters, Kristie, Tammy, and Bonny. They are my friends, my prayer partners, my encouragers, my counselors, and my helpers. They are and always have been wonderful children. Even when I neglected them for their brother's problems and for other things such as my mother and church projects, they still loved me through it all.

To my three wonderful sons-in-law who love God and me, for whom I am so thankful.

To my beautiful grandchildren, who are such a joy and delight in my life.

To Bill and Ginger Behrman, the wonderful pastors who kept us anchored in Jesus as we went through the mighty rough waters of our lives.

Each one of these people I love very much, and I thank God for them.

Acknowledgments

A number of people played roles in enabling this book to become a reality. Thanks to . . .

J.D., my husband, for his love, encouragement, support, and patience, and for all of his typing.

Kristie, my daughter, for choosing the title and some other parts, for her many hours of typing and editing, and for her love, encouragement, and prayers.

Tammy, my daughter, for helping with the cover and for her many hours of typing, editing, love, encouragement, and prayers.

Bonny, my daughter, for the special book and pens used for all my notes and for her many hours of typing and editing, and for her love, encouragement, and prayers.

Charlie, Jeff, and Len (my sons-in-law), for their typing and editing, and for their patience, love, and prayers.

Austin and Julia (my grandchildren), for all of their patience, love, and prayers.

Iola, my mother, for all of her love, prayers, and support.

All my family and friends, for their prayers.

McDougal Publishing, for editing, typesetting and publishing this book.

CONTENTS

Introduction

Have you ever gone through a day or maybe many days as a child or as an adult that you wondered if you had a sign over you — a sign that said: "Pick on me. Be rude to me. Be mean and ugly to me"? Is that the kind of treatment you receive from many people who are around you? If so, you may have a generational curse over you. You may have received this curse at birth as an unwanted gift.

Maybe your child lies or steals, but you have always been very honest. You wonder, how did my child get this way? Maybe it came to the child as an unwanted gift from a grandfather or from a great grandmother.

> *I the LORD thy God am a jealous God, visiting the iniquity of the fathers upon the children unto the third and fourth generation of them that hate me.*   Exodus 20:5

There is good news! Such curses can be broken and reversed for you, for your children, and for your grandchildren forever. You can break the curse over their lives with the blood of the Lord Jesus Christ.

Christ hath redeemed us from the curse of the law, being made a curse for us: for it is written, Cursed is every one that hangeth on a tree. Galatians 3:13

Know therefore that the LORD *thy God, he is God, the faithful God, which keepeth covenant and mercy with them that love him and keep his commandments to a thousand generations.* Deuteronomy 7:9

The curse is broken by the name that is above every name, the name of Jesus. We are set free by the precious shed blood of our Lord Jesus and by speaking what God says about our situation.

And they overcame him by the blood of the Lamb, and by the word of their testimony. Revelation 12:11

We are set free through the power of the Holy Spirit, our helper, our comforter, our strength, and guide, and through the written word of God.

Now thanks be unto God, which always causeth us to triumph in Christ. Second Corinthians 2:14

Christians have gifts that allow them to over-come. We can walk in the overcomer's blessing!

I pray this book will bring glory to God. It is all about Him. Its purpose is to lift up the name of Jesus, because He said,

> *And I, if I be lifted up from the earth, will draw all men unto me.* John 12:32

I pray that the blood of the Lamb and the word of your testimony will set you free. I pray that you will be set free to serve Jesus. I pray that you will be filled with the precious Holy Spirit and covered by His anointing. And I pray that you will be filled with God's love and mercy and His Word, and that you will walk in the blessed Gift He has given you for your new birth.

Ramona Duffield
Ashland, Virginia

CHAPTER ONE

GENERATIONAL GIFTS

There are gifts that we receive in the spirit from our parents and give to our children at birth. These gifts may be blessings, or they may be curses. To begin this book, I will share part of my life and from my son's life too. My testimony and his story will help illustrate the lesson of generational gifts, whether they be curses or blessings.

A while back, my sister told me that she had prayed to have a baby sister. She remembers looking into the baby basket after I was born and being happy to see me, the answer to her prayer. When she prayed for me to come, she couldn't have imagined how much prayer I would need throughout my life. I thank God for my praying sister and for a praying mother, too. I know I would not be here today if it had not been for the prayers of my mother, sister, and grandmother. I thank God that my birth gift was the blessing of prayer.

When I was three months old, I almost died. My mother, my sister, and my grandmother prayed me through and I lived. My brother also prayed for me as he grew older. My brother and I were the best of friends while we were growing up and still are today.

As a teenager I became rebellious in a quiet sort of way, but quiet or not, it was rebellion. I wanted to live for God, but I wanted to do it my way. My mother read the Bible and prayed with us every night, so I never stopped praying and asking God for help, but I wasn't willing to separate myself from sin.

I was raped at age fourteen, which led me into a life of promiscuity. I can say that I chose to stay in that lifestyle, and by age fifteen I found myself pregnant. Between the fourth and fifth month, I was sent to a large city a few hours away supposedly to attend a church camp, or so my parents thought. Actually, I planned to go have an abortion.

Abortions were illegal at that time, and many girls died as victims of backstreet abortions. I know it may sound stupid on my part, but I never once thought of abortion as murder. I was just doing what I had been told to do. But the father of my child, who was going to help me with the abortion, didn't come and meet me as planned.

I got back on the bus and went home. In August, I was seven months pregnant. This time the father of the life inside of me put me on a bus to another city. I was going to go to a home for unwed mothers and to arrange for the adoption of my baby.

When I arrived, I went to the first hotel I could find. I wasn't familiar with the city. I was given a room on the thirteenth floor. I never felt so alone in my life, and as I stood before that window looking down on that city, I cried out to God and said, "If You're there, God, and if You care, please help me."

I called the father of my child the next day. He came to the hotel and told me I had to go to the home for unwed mothers. He knew my family was worried sick and that I had just disappeared. I had left home just two days before the appointment my mother had made for me to see a doctor about the "tumor" I was developing.

So he told me to call my sister, which I did. She came immediately, borrowing the money from her little boy's piggy bank to be able to make the trip. Shortly after that, her husband and my dad came also. My dad told me that I would never be able to live with myself if I gave my baby away. He was right.

I thank God my dad came at that time. I have never ever been sorry that I kept my child. We went home, and my baby, Bruce, was born November tenth. The doctor thought the baby came about two weeks late. He was a very beautiful baby, and he was whole in every way, which was an answer to my prayers.

About fifteen months before, while I was in my state of rebellion, I had met a very special young man. I had seen him for only about an hour, and I had refused to talk to him. I spoke to him no more at that time. After my baby was born, God brought him to my mind, and I prayed for six months that if he was the right husband for me and the right daddy for my baby, he would come down to where I lived, which was about two hundred miles away from his home.

So when he came one day, I knew I would marry him, although he didn't yet. Our pastor's wife brought us together through God's guidance. I thank God for the pastor and his wife. They helped me to put the guilt behind me and to go on living.

The special young man and I were married three and one-half months later. I was sixteen and he was twenty. What a prince of a husband he was and still is! Everyone knew it. My aunt still says that if she could just find a man like J.D., she would marry him. We have had, and still have, a wonderful marriage. I thank God for such a wonderful husband, and daddy for my children.

We moved to the city he was living in, and my husband adopted Bruce a year later. We had three beautiful daughters, each of whom I felt was a miracle and a gift from God. I also had two miscarriages during this time. In 1976 we moved to a small town, and life went on. We were very happy.

CHAPTER TWO

LOVE IS BLIND

At birth Bruce received curses that were seen while he was still very young. At age five he was caught stealing candy from a store. He also became a master at lying at a very early age.

When he was thirteen years old, our dog died. He loved that dog very much. He said the dog was the brother he never had. Bruce sat by the dog's side, praying for him. The dog died a very awful death; he was poisoned. It took three days for the animal to die.

He also had a lot of older friends who moved away, including the director of education at our church, whom he idolized. Later, our youth pastor left, and the singing group he was in broke up because it was left without a leader. His best friend, a Christian boy at school, moved away too.

As time passed, he looked for new friends elsewhere, but he found the wrong kind. He got involved in drugs, alcohol, theft, and sex. We were very concerned for him, and for our girls, after finding alcohol under his mattress. We thought to ask him to leave home, but God told us just to love him, so we did. We prayed a lot for him. I kept thinking that maybe someone would help him. Maybe he would go on a retreat or to a camp or to some other meeting.

God spoke to my heart and said that He would perfect that which concerns me (see Psalm 138:8). I understood that He would perfect our son, and that it would not be the work of man. We stood on that verse, but Bruce continued doing his own thing. I know that he wanted to do right and to please us. He loved us, but he seemed unable to do what he knew he should.

In the fall of 1982, I was praying on a Sunday evening before church. We had prayer at five o'clock in the morning six days a week, and on Sunday evening before church also. This particular evening I went into very deep intercession for our son. I could not describe the pain I felt within. This happened to me again later during the service, and the whole church prayed. I saw myself in that hotel room when I was fifteen years old and so very alone, crying out for help.

At first, I saw myself standing before the window. Then I saw Bruce. Afterwards I could see someone standing there crying out for help, but there wasn't any face. I asked God who it was. I felt such a burden for this faceless person. The Lord told me, "It is many."

About four years before this, the Lord had spoken to my husband and me about working with young people. I felt He was confirming this calling again, laying the many on our hearts.

I remember, when Bruce was about fifteen years old, a special young lady was preaching on Sunday morning at our church, and she called him to come forward with a few other boys for an illustration. She had the other boys be the devil, one covering Bruce's eyes and the other covering his ears, and we in the congregation were supposed to intercede until we got the devil off of him. The text that the minister was illustrating was:

> [I] *cease not to give thanks for you, making mention of you in my prayers; that the God of our Lord Jesus Christ, the Father of glory, may give unto you the spirit of wisdom and revelation in the knowledge of him: the eyes of your understanding being enlightened; that ye may know what is the hope of his calling, and what the riches of the glory of his inheritance in the saints, and what is the exceeding greatness of his power to us-ward who believe, according to the working of his*

mighty power, which he wrought in Christ, when he raised him from the dead, and set him at his own right hand in the heavenly places. Ephesians 1:16-20

Bruce moved repeatedly during his sixteenth and seventeenth years. He moved away, and then came back home often, but most of the time he was away from us.

That fall, when he was making one of his moves, God told me to type Proverbs 1:10-19 on a paper and to put the paper in his suitcase. This was a warning to him from God. As I look back, it seems that it may also have been a warning to me:

My son, if sinners entice thee, consent thou not. If they say, Come with us, let us lay wait for blood, let us lurk privily for the innocent without cause: let us swallow them up alive as the grave; and whole, as those that go down into the pit: we shall find all precious substance, we shall fill our houses with spoil: cast in thy lot among us; let us all have one purse: my son, walk not thou in the way with them; refrain thy foot from their path: for their feet run to evil, and make haste to shed blood. Surely in vain the net is spread in the sight of any bird. And they lay wait for their own blood; they lurk privily for their own lives. So are the ways of every one that is greedy of gain; which taketh away the life of the owners thereof. Proverbs 1:10-19

Our son told me later he read it and wanted to do what was right, but he was so entangled in sin and with the wrong people. He couldn't see any way out.

I believe this illustration and text also provided a warning to us, and we did pray, but not as much as we should have and not until Christ was fully formed in him.

Bruce had turned eighteen in November, and in December he was trying hard to find a job. Later that same month he went to a city a few hours away. He said he had applied for thirty different jobs, but wasn't able to get one. He even tried to join the Army, but as of January the Army had begun to require a high school diploma, and Bruce had dropped out of school, so he couldn't join.

Bruce came home very discouraged. On February second his girlfriend broke up with him. February fourth he came home about five o'clock in the morning. My husband and I were awake, praying. He said he was going to a city a few hours away.

At nine-thirty in the morning, Bruce and his friend came back home, and they were very tired and depressed. He said that they had been unable to get the car started and that they had nearly frozen in the cold. It was eight degrees below zero that night.

They went to take a nap, but couldn't sleep. That afternoon (Thursday), my husband called from work saying that two people were dead and that Bruce had better have a good explanation of where he had been the night before, because Bruce and his friend had associated with the victims.

That night, just before we left to watch our daughter in the school's play, the police came and talked to Bruce. I was so troubled inside that I asked God for a scripture for Bruce and his friend. God gave me this verse.

> *I will lift up mine eyes unto the hills, from whence cometh my help. My help cometh from the LORD, which made heaven and earth. He will not suffer thy foot to be moved: he that keepeth thee will not slumber. Behold, he that keepeth Israel shall neither slumber nor sleep. The LORD is thy keeper; the LORD is thy shade upon thy right hand. The sun shall not smite thee by day, nor the moon by night. The LORD shall preserve thee from all evil: he shall preserve thy soul. The LORD shall preserve thy going out and thy coming in from this time forth, and even for evermore.*
> Psalm 121

I was so thankful for the scripture, but I did not interpret all of it correctly.

On Friday morning I went to the video Bible classes we were having at our church. I told our pastor on the way downstairs that I needed to talk to him (thinking he would talk to me later), but he immediately went upstairs to his office and I followed.

I told him that the police had come, and he prayed with me. After the class, our pastor and his wife came over and talked with Bruce. After they left, Bruce turned to me and said, "What am I going to do about the mess I am in? No one can help me now."

I said, "Don't you think that the God who created this universe, the heavens and the earth is able to help you if you turn your life over to Him."

He said, "Yes, I guess He will."

Then Bruce went upstairs and prayed, and he made a commitment to God.

I really had no idea what kind of a mess he was talking about. My love for my son had blinded me. That Saturday we had a wonderful day as a family. We played games, and then we went to a meeting about fifty miles away. We sang songs as we traveled. The preacher spoke on the theme of knowing and trusting our Father God.

I heard Bruce pray in the spirit for the first time in a long while. We had such a wonderful day. It was a day to be remembered. We did not know that things would never be quite the same thereafter.

The police questioned our son three times that week. On Wednesday, February 9, 1983, which was just a week later, Bruce received a letter from my nephew. I never read my children's mail, but this day I did. It was a letter telling him about his natural father, whose obituary was enclosed (he had died in an accident when Bruce was one month old).

We had told Bruce some things, but we did not tell him everything. He had always had many unanswered questions. He had finally decided to go back to school, so after school I gave him the letter and answered all his questions. I was so thankful I was able to do so that day.

We all went to church that night. After church, Bruce ate supper because he had not eaten before church. I sat and talked with him while he ate. I then went upstairs to read, and I prayed with the girls and put them to bed.

The doorbell rang, and J.D. called me. As I rushed downstairs, I saw Bruce with his wrists handcuffed behind his back being led out of our front door. My heart sank.

An officer from the Colorado Bureau of Investigation said they were arresting him on two counts of first-degree murder. When they left, my husband helped me to sit down. He told the girls and called our pastors and they came immediately.

Chapter Three

The Arrest

Our pastors cried and prayed with us as we sobbed for a long time. My family went to bed, but I prayed and talked with my Father God until dawn, asking about the things He had told us, if they were all true or if they were all lies. I felt that I had to believe all that God had said or turn my back on everything. It wasn't a hard choice. I loved and believed God, and I knew He was the only One who could help us now.

I wondered if we should move. I wanted to flee from there, but we couldn't leave our son. As the light in the eastern sky began to rise, God spoke these words to my spirit:

MY GRACE IS SUFFICIENT FOR THEE: for my strength is made perfect in weakness.
Second Corinthians 12:9

I got up and went to bed for a little while. We went ahead and sent the girls to school that day, knowing it would be harder if they waited. A couple of kids said something to our youngest daughter, who was seven at the time. Her teacher, who was a Christian, had taught Bruce and really liked him. She tried to stop the other kids from saying anything bad to her.

When our second daughter was to start school, I waited until she was six years old, feeling that was a better time for her to start, and I had planned to do the same with our youngest, but the Lord spoke to my heart and told me to send her when she was five years old. I had done so, and I believe it was so she would have that teacher at that time, and maybe for other reasons also.

Our second daughter was eleven and one-half years old at the time, and she was in middle school. The principal's son liked our daughter, and the principal's wife had taught Bruce. So the principal was very supportive and protective of her. Even so, some terrible things were said to her. Our oldest daughter, who was almost fifteen years old, was in high school. A few kids and a teacher said something very hurtful to her, but another girl, one she really didn't know well, wrote her a letter telling her she would have to be the strong one in the family in light of what had happened and that she would be someone we could all lean on. From that point on, she stood strong.

Each of our girls was wonderful through the whole time. They never let the incident affect their grades or their work, and especially they remained strong in their stand for Christ. We thank God for His protection and for each of the people He used to help our children through the difficult time.

We received three ugly phone calls with the caller calling us *murderers.* I was saddened to find that our oldest daughter was on the line too and heard everything. But God helped her, and He helped us. I told my sister about the phone calls, and she prayed they would stop. Afterwards we never had another one!

God gave us several portions from Psalms:

> *Thou shalt hide them in the secret of thy presence from the pride of man: thou shalt keep them secretly in a pavilion from the strife of tongues. Blessed be the LORD: for he hath shewed me his marvellous kindness in a strong city.* Psalm 31:20-21

> *But let all those that put their trust in thee rejoice: let them ever shout for joy, because thou defendest them: let them also that love thy name be joyful in thee. For thou, LORD, wilt*

bless the righteous; with favour wilt thou compass him as with a shield.

Psalm 5:11-12

My defence is of God, which saveth the upright in heart. Psalm 7:10

The morning after Bruce's arrest, our pastors came over again. They visited us many times in the days and months and years that followed. We have repeatedly and continually thanked God for our pastors. They were the best pastors anyone could ever have. They encouraged us always, and gave us counsel without putting us down or condemning us. They were just as supportive of our son.

Many times we experienced fears about the future, but they prayed with us. They gave us scriptures for us to stand on and to relieve our fears. Our pastors informed our church family, and they came and brought food. I don't remember the words that many of them spoke to us, but they were there with us, and that was important. Many called, and others wrote to us. Not only did our church family support us, but also our immediate families as well. Also, many friends we had met over the years called or wrote, providing tremendous support throughout the entire time.

I remember the first person who came to visit us besides our pastors. She was a very dear, sweet lady in the church, and she hugged me tight. We cried together. Everyone was such a blessing, and most of all, they prayed, and they carried us through this awful time.

That next morning, after Bruce's arrest, I found that my body would go into shaking spells. I suppose it was the shock. Some friends and family thought I should see a doctor, but I didn't want to. I wanted just one thing, and that was to see Bruce.

We were finally allowed in to see Bruce that afternoon. It was so wonderful to see him. We had to visit with guards watching and listening to us, but it was still so wonderful to be with him again.

As we left that day, he asked us to go buy him some cigarettes. This was something we had never done before. He asked us to bring them back to him before we read the letter he gave us, the one that he had written to us as we sat there.

I guess he thought we might not come back, but we told him that no matter what the letter said, we would always love him and stand beside him through it all — *not standing for the wrong, but standing in love and compassion and forgiveness towards him.*

Every day we tried to see him and give him a hug. It meant so much! On Sunday we had to visit him standing behind a screen. It was so awful! We visited him every moment they allowed. For the first week, we visited nearly every day. Then they reduced the visits to three days, and finally they allowed us only two days a week.

During this time God gave us many scriptures. We went to the Word daily and went over these scriptures and many others. We did this twice and sometimes three times a day. We also spent time in our Father God's presence, in fellowship with Him. This sustained us. This time in His presence became our strength and our life.

Cast thy burden upon the LORD, and he shall sustain thee: he shall never suffer the righteous to be moved. Psalm 55:22

He that dwelleth in the secret place of the most High shall abide under the shadow of the Almighty. I will say of the LORD, He is my refuge and my fortress: my God; in him will I trust. Surely he shall deliver thee from the snare of the fowler, and from the noisome pestilence. He shall cover thee with his feathers, and under his wings shalt thou trust: his truth shall be thy shield and buckler. Thou shalt not be afraid for the terror by night; nor for the arrow that flieth by day; nor for the pestilence that walketh in darkness; nor for the destruction that wasteth at noonday. A thousand shall fall at thy side, and ten thousand at thy right hand; but it shall not come nigh thee. Only with thine eyes shalt thou behold and see the reward of the wicked. Because thou hast made the LORD, which is my refuge, even the most High, thy habitation; there shall no evil befall thee, neither shall any plague come nigh thy dwelling. For he shall give his angels charge over thee, to keep thee in all thy ways. They shall bear thee up in their hands, lest thou dash thy foot against a stone. Thou shalt tread upon the lion and adder: the young lion and the dragon shalt thou trample under feet. Because he hath set his love upon me, therefore will I deliver him: I will set him on high, because he hath known my name. He shall call upon me, and I will answer him: I will be with him in trouble; I will deliver him, and honour him. With long life will I satisfy him, and shew him my salvation.

Psalms 91

He will regard the prayer of the destitute, and not despise their prayer. This shall be written for the generation to come: and the people which shall be created shall praise the LORD. For he hath looked down from the height of his sanctuary; from heaven did the LORD be-

hold the earth; to hear the groaning of the prisoner; to loose those that are appointed to death. Psalm 102:17-20

So shall they fear the name of the LORD from the west, and his glory from the rising of the sun. When the enemy shall come in like a flood, the Spirit of the LORD shall lift up a standard against him.
And the Redeemer shall come to Zion, and unto them that turn from transgression in Jacob, saith the LORD. As for me, this is my covenant with them, saith the LORD; My spirit that is upon thee, and my words which I have put in thy mouth, shall not depart out of thy mouth, nor out of the mouth of thy seed, nor out of the mouth of thy seed's seed, saith the LORD, from henceforth and for ever. Isaiah 59:19-21

Some of these scriptures speak about favor. God gave us favor with the jailers and with everyone we came in contact with. Some of the verses talk about protection, some about strength, some about guidance, and others about protection from gossip and strife of tongues. God granted us all of these. He blessed us daily and helped us.

We prayed for Bruce to have another blanket, and he was given it. We prayed for him to have an extra pillow, and he was given it. We even prayed for him to be given an extra mattress and he was given it. We prayed for extra time during visits and calls, for better rooms for our visits, and that he could have things we brought to him. All of these requests were granted, and more. I was even allowed to do his laundry. This meant so much to me and to him. I also cut his hair, and that was a real blessing too.

CHAPTER FOUR

RELEASED

During the first part of March, Bruce was moved in the middle of the night to another town. It was about seventy-five miles away. The officers hadn't told us about the move, and it wasn't until I took something for him the next day that I found out.

It was a hard time for the whole family. We were not allowed to visit him. After some days we were allowed to visit, but a blizzard kept us from traveling. Yet even in this, God worked everything to our good.

After the blizzard was over, we were allowed to visit and to take his high school work to him. He was working on completing his GED. Ordinarily, we were only allowed to visit through a glass window, but this time we visited with him in the same room and were able to explain his schoolwork, since we were given fifteen minutes to visit, rather than five. We were able to give him a hug, which ended up having to last us over a month and a half, until he was moved elsewhere.

In the new facility we were able to visit him once a week, but we had to speak through a phone and were separated by a glass window. It was very hard! Bruce would put his hand on one side of the glass, and we would put hands up to his although separated by the barrier.

As the weeks passed, God gave us more time with him, and on several occasions they allowed J.D. and me both fifteen and twenty minutes with our son, and the girls were allowed to visit with us, too.

In March, I prayed God would tell me what was going to happen. (That is not always a good thing to ask!) A lady in our church gave me a letter. The letter explained a dream she had about what was going to happen to Bruce. She had the dream in February. It was so difficult for me to handle, and everything developed just like the dream had indicated. The dream did not give an exact answer in words; rather, it was spiritual and had to be discerned. In the dream there were concrete walls, but the lady who had the dream couldn't reach Bruce, though she knew he was okay. She saw things getting better, a little at a time, and love expanded as if it was a ripple moving across the water. The thick concrete walls concerned me though. I was hoping that he wouldn't go to prison, for up until now he had only been in county jails.

One day at the end of April we spent a very long day in court. They said it would take an hour, or at the most an hour and a half, but it went from 10:00 AM to 7:00 PM. It was a terrible day. When it was over, I just wanted to run and run into a wheat field that was tall with wheat and lie down and cry and never come out. When I was a kid, I hid in the wheat fields where I could escape from the world at times.

Bruce wanted to commit suicide, but God ministered to him in his cell. Our dear, wonderful pastors came and took J.D. and me to another town for dinner. It was Wednesday and they never missed church, but that night they left the ninety and nine to minister to us (the one).

They ministered to us so much! We were about as low as we could go, both emotionally and physically, and we were drained. God lifted us up through them. They encouraged us and said we would have the ministry God promised us. When it happened, it would happen just as though God had snapped His fingers.

My sister said she heard on the radio that there was a rainbow over our town that day. (She lives in a different town.) That was a reminder to us that God's Word and promises were still yea and amen.

After that day, Bruce was moved back to our town. My husband and I started walking and praying in our usual prayer time at 5:00 AM. We would walk around the courthouse, which had the jail in the top of it, twice every morning and on some mornings more times. We had a little dog Bruce loved that we would take on the walk with us. Bruce would light a match and hold it up in the window to let us know that he was praying too. This was a wonderful point of contact.

The jailers got in the habit of waking him up at five o'clock so he wouldn't miss us. Again, God gave us favor. In November we were even allowed to have a birthday party for Bruce. It was his nineteenth birthday. Nineteen of us attended. We brought gifts and a homemade cake (his favorite), but to Bruce the best part was that we all had communion together, which our pastor served. Bruce was right in his heart with God. He said it was the best birthday he ever had or ever would have.

The day we celebrated was not his actual birthday. When I had called on the day of his birthday, I had prayed we would be granted extra time to speak. The person in charge of the time had had a meeting and forgot about us! We talked for two hours.

> *Whatsoever ye shall ask the Father in my name, he will give it you. ... Ask, and ye shall receive, that your joy may be full.*
>
> John 16:23-24

During all this, Bruce prayed sometimes for up to two hours a day, and he saw nine or more other prisoners accept Jesus as their Savior and several of them also filled with the Holy Spirit. He had a part in helping them find Jesus, along with the pastors who visited.

In the first part of November, Bruce accepted a plea bargain for one twelve-year sentence or six years with good behavior, and less with earned time. Since he had been facing the possibility of one hundred five years, or even the death penalty, it was a wonderful miracle. We really thanked God for it!

At that time there were things that I really didn't know. The lawyers told us not to talk to Bruce about the case because the prosecution could force us to speak, but they couldn't force Bruce to say anything. I had thought we would go to court and Bruce would be freed, so I was devastated when it didn't happen that way. Our pastors tried to prepare me, but I wasn't ready.

The day Bruce called to tell us he had accepted the plea bargain, I thought I would die. The past ten months had been like one terrible, long day, yet divided into a thousand days that never ended. And now this!

Later that day, J.D. went somewhere. He put a tape on before he left. My husband has been my greatest supporter, and he helped me through this trial and helped me to stay next to the Lord. I have the greatest husband! I was lying on the floor when the speaker on the tape that J.D. had left said something about getting up and going on with God in the middle of impossible circumstances. I do not even know what tape it was, but I praise God for the ministry of the Holy Spirit through it. God really ministered to me through that tape.

> *God is our refuge and strength, a very present help in trouble.* Psalm 46:1

Though I still had a hard time for a while, I had a dream. In the dream we were in a room talking about something very depressing. We were on the sofa with a bunch of people in the room, but the only ones I remember were my husband sitting beside me and our pastors across from us. The dream was so depressing that I suddenly stood up in it and threw my arm back and shouted:

> *For God hath not given us the spirit of fear; but of power, and of love, and of a sound mind.* Second Timothy 1:7

Then I sat down and the people in my dream started laughing. I said, "Well, I needed that!" Then I woke up and said the verse again.

I got up, but that scripture kept going through my mind over and over again. I prayed silently a while, and then I went back to bed.

Shortly after that incident, I called a ministry Bruce had asked me to call so I could ask for prayer.

After I got off the phone I fell apart. I asked, "Oh, God, what is happening to me?"

I felt like I was losing my sanity, and the dream returned to me. I responded the same way, with Second Timothy 1:7, for I knew it was God's promise to me!

By the time December came, there was a man in jail who kept trying to get Bruce to fight him, but Bruce wouldn't do it. One night the man who had been threatening our son beat him up and bashed his head against the cement floor many times, until his face swelled so much that it split the skin.

He called us at 1:00 AM to tell us they had just sewed him up at the hospital. That was on Friday night. We could not see him until Monday, and his face was still black and blue and swollen so much that he could barely open his eye. I thank God he did not lose his eye or his life.

The first of February Bruce was sentenced, and he was moved to a state prison. Up until this point he had been in the county jail. The first night in the penitentiary was really awful for him. It was so full that there wasn't any room for him, so they put him in the maximum security "hole" for the night.

Within two weeks he was moved again. We knew he had been moved, but we didn't know where. They said he would call, but they didn't allow him to make any calls for three months. I called the next day, and at least found out where they had taken him. Later he was in an accident, or so they said. They thought someone had pushed him out of a pickup truck that was taking some of the men to their jobs in the prison. He fell on the same side of his face that had been injured earlier.

He went into convulsions and almost swallowed his tongue three times. His work detail boss used a comb to keep him from choking on it. He was in the hospital for a day. We visited him a few days later. It was a real shock to see him walk in all bandaged up. We knew nothing about what had happened until we saw him. We thanked God he was alive. God always protected him from all the attempts on his life in prison and from some other attempts after he was out.

> *For the sighing of the needy, now will I arise, saith the LORD; I will set him in safety from him that puffeth at him.* Psalm 12:5

Every move in the system was very traumatic for all of us, but things did get better for him as he went through it, and for us too. In some places the rules were harder for us because the rules changed from place to place, but with every move came some sort of improvement. During the whole time that Bruce was in prison, God allowed us to visit him about once every two weeks, and sometimes more often. We had to travel six to ten hours for every visit. We thank God we were able to go that often, for it helped hold our family together.

We also thank God for protecting us through all those travels.

> *There shall no evil befall thee, neither shall any plague come nigh thy dwelling.*
>   Psalm 91:10

Bruce always had jobs in the prison that he liked. He did construction work, cement work, maintenance work, and some office work. At one place he did maintenance, and he even had his own room with a kitchen and a large recreation room that he shared with three others. He did his own cooking, and there was a patio. We had a family barbecue, and could bring most any kind of food from home. God gave us much favor everywhere we went.

About six months before his release he got weekend furloughs, so we went more often then. The Christmas before he was released we were allowed a special one-day pass, and we were able to bring him home on Saturday.

Thus saith the LORD; Refrain thy voice from weeping, and thine eyes from tears: for thy work shall be rewarded, saith the LORD; and they shall come again from the land of the enemy. And there is hope in thine end, saith the LORD, that thy children shall come again to their own border. Jeremiah 31:16-17

It was wonderful to have him home for that day. Bruce spent five years and three months in prison, so he was released early.

CHAPTER FIVE

ONLY HIS GRACE

The day came for Bruce's release from prison, and we rejoiced in that. We took a short family trip. It was a special time for Bruce. He was off of parole one year after he was released, and he worked at an elevator, and worked in construction too.

He met a nice little gal, and they were married in September. They didn't have much money, and we didn't either, but God helped us give them a very lovely wedding. Everyone in our family helped with it. It was our gift to them.

In late November they found out that they were expecting a baby. Bruce was elated. His wife wanted to wait until Christmas to tell everyone, but he was so excited about being a daddy that he couldn't wait. We were glad to share in his excitement and good news.

They came to our house for Thanksgiving and we had such a wonderful time. All of the children went together and bought a Christmas tree. They decorated it together. Bruce and his wife saw our new church. At the end of November I had lunch with them again, at my mom and dad's home, and we had a beautiful time.

It was December 10, 1989, a Sunday, and early that morning the doorbell rang. It was our pastor. I was still in bed, and J.D. ran up the stairs to get me. He told me that the pastor had come and that he thought he had some bad news; he wanted us to come quickly.

I threw on a robe and went downstairs. Our pastor put his arms around both of us. He said there had been a wreck the night before and Bruce had been killed.

I fell to the floor, sobbing. I was overcome. My husband and my pastor laid hands on me and prayed in the Spirit. After a few minutes I began to feel great strength and peace.

I knew Bruce was safe in the arms of Jesus. No one could ever hurt him again. The devil could not ever touch him again, and he was free from all of his fears.

He had been so afraid for us. He had been waking up with nightmares, desperately speaking, "Oh, they've got my family! They've got my family."

I was concerned about our oldest daughter, who was in a Bible college twelve hours away without any family there. I got up and called her. God sustained her, and the family of God reached out to her. The Lord sustained all of us, and the body of Christ reached out to us in love with their prayers and their support. They donated both food and finances to our family. We were blessed with so much!

Our church and the women's group paid to fly our oldest daughter home. We were so thankful that she didn't have to drive home alone. We could feel the prayers and the support coming from many for days and months thereafter.

Is it a mystery to me why Bruce died? No, not at all. The Holy Spirit led me to the answer in God's Word.

My little children, of whom I travail in birth
again until Christ be formed in you...
Galatians 4:19

We didn't do this. It is true that we spent much time in prayer for him, but we did not *travail in birth again until Christ was formed* in our son. We really didn't have the understanding that we needed to have travailed for him.

He found himself doing the wrong things even when he wanted to do right. Much of his failure surely came to him as a result of the curses he inherited at birth. The negative birthday presents that fell to him made the victorious life difficult for him.

Did we abuse him? No, we did not. I believe that children conceived out of marriage are abused already, because they are born without the covering that God instituted. I believe this makes them even more vulnerable to the curse of inheritance from the "fathers" than the rest of us. Curses were passed down to Bruce's biological father and grandfather, which also came to him. His grandfather was an alcoholic. His father had sexually abused other girls besides me, also leaving them pregnant, and he also lusted after pornography.

Not only did Bruce receive curses from his biological father, but he also received curses on the day of his birth that were from my side. Both my mother and my father had been physically abused during their lifetimes, though not by their own parents. My dad had also been sexually abused with pornography during his time in an orphanage. I had been sexually abused as a teenager, as I've already testified in these pages, and this is something that everyone knew about, but I was also sexually abused as a child. Almost nobody knew, and I never wanted anyone to know.

The source of this abuse had been someone outside of our home. It happened several times when I was a little girl, and a couple of other times as I grew up. I have been told that I was also physically abused when I was nine months old. I do not remember that instance. I also had been through a lot of mental abuse as a child. Once you have been abused, a spirit attaches itself to you and doesn't let go. To be delivered from it, you must apply the blood of Jesus and face the situation or sin and deal directly with it. If you don't do that, it will keep coming back.

Bruce also was abused as a small child by a neighbor and another time when he was a teenager. That spirit didn't let go.

Bruce had made some really bad choices when he first got out of prison. He needed to go to where he could get some spiritual growth and structure, but he fell back into contact with the wrong crowd and again became involved with alcohol and sex.

I was warned of God to pray more or things would not go right, and I did pray more, but not with consistency. In May, I had felt led of the Lord to go and get our son. So I had prayed a great deal on the way to the town where he lived. It was three hours away. I knew he wouldn't want to come with me. Sure enough, he was angry and didn't want to come with me, but I had felt strongly that he would die if he didn't leave then.

When I reached him, I told him that he had to leave then and that I knew he would die if he didn't. If he wanted to come back later, that was up to him, but I told him he had to leave then. He finally agreed, though he insisted that he had things to do in town before he left. As we went to take care of the details he wanted to attend to, we were followed everywhere. He had been followed for several days already. We managed to ditch the one who was following us. I know God's protection was there that day.

> *For he shall give his angels charge over thee,*
> *to keep thee in all thy ways.*   Psalm 91:11

I took Bruce to a small town in a nearby state, and he didn't move back to the city I helped him leave. But he lived in fear, and rightfully so. His lifestyle caused him many close calls. He told us that he had been involved in organized crime, and though he never mentioned any names or places or other details, he told us it was a large group and that there was no escape from it. He told us that sometimes people who tried to get out of the group moved suddenly or died mysteriously.

Somehow, he had made contact with them again. When you are trying to live for God but walk in sin, God still loves you, but sin separates you from God's protection and from His promises. *For the wages of sin is death* (Romans 6:23).

> *I have set before you life and death, blessing*
> *and cursing: therefore choose life.*
>   Deuteronomy 30:19

Ultimately, because of his lifestyle, Bruce chose death. If the curses he had received on the day of his birth had been broken, I believe he would have made different choices in life.

When he had married in September, he became the head of his home, but he was not ready for this and his house was not fully covered. The enemy was still able to enter in because Bruce was clinging to sin, even though he tried to live for God. We are only covered when we walk uprightly and stand upon the Word and upon the blood of Jesus.

Many things happened after his marriage before the end came. He broke his heel, he cut his hand, he cut his back very badly, a nail shot him in the eye (but it didn't blind him), he fell, his wife nearly lost the baby, and the doctor wanted to abort the baby — just to name a few. Bruce was buffeted by Satan because he didn't resist evil and walk firmly for Christ.

I fell into fear myself in November. I told God that if Bruce wasn't going to be ready for the Rapture, to please take him at a time when he would be ready. I should not have fallen into fear. I already had God's promise:

> *Being confident of this very thing, that he which hath begun a good work in you will perform it until the day of Jesus Christ.*
>
> Philippians 1:6

I shouldn't have prayed such a prayer when I already had the promise of God. He said He would complete the work He began, and I should have trusted Him for that work. God has forgiven me, and our son is safe and he is secure with Jesus. I knew he was in Heaven because God spoke to my heart. He was spiritually immature, but he was there.

Sometimes the devil tries to put thoughts in your head. I knew Bruce was reading his Bible daily and praying daily, but I also knew that alcohol still had its grip on his life. So I asked God to confirm to me that he was in Heaven. In response, God allowed me to hear from two people who had dreams or visions. One saw him, as an eight-year-old boy, sitting on Jesus' lap, and Jesus had His arms around him.

The other person saw him lying in a room full of trash. He then got up off the floor and climbed the stairs. At the top of the stairs he turned and told the person having the dream that he had made it to the top (to Heaven).

My sister bought me a plaque with Bruce's name on it. The plaque said that his name meant safe and secure. I know he is safe and secure with Jesus.

We believe Bruce must have had some help out of this world. There was evidence of a second vehicle as indicated by the vehicle tracks and a mark on the pickup truck he was driving. Both clues seem to indicate that foul play was involved. He also had called his wife and had asked her to pray. He was afraid he wasn't going to make it home that night.

I do not have unforgiveness in my heart towards anyone though at one time I did towards some of the people our son had gotten mixed up with, because they had involved him in a wayward lifestyle. For a time I even resented the police, because I felt that if they had done their job and had stopped the people who had been involved in illegal activity for years (activity which the police knew about) Bruce would still be alive. At a retreat I attended, God healed my heart and took away all the unforgiveness that had been in my heart. Praise God!

The devil did not win. God did! Bruce is with God. The scripture that God gave me in the beginning was true:

My grace is sufficient for thee: for my strength is made perfect in weakness.
Second Corinthians 12:9

God's supernatural sustaining power, love, favor and wisdom were more than enough for us. *Only His grace* could have brought us through this trial. We had the supernatural grace of God to support us through impossible circumstances.

One day after Bruce went to be with Jesus, I found that I was having a difficult time accepting what had happened and I was praying. At that time I felt impressed to read some of the old letters he had sent me. I argued with this quickening, feeling that it could only make things worse for me, but I kept feeling this need so strongly that I went ahead and began reading.

One of the first letters that I picked up almost immediately gave me peace. It was a good letter. In it, one of the scriptures Bruce had written was :

For our light affliction, which is but for a moment, worketh for us a far more exceeding and eternal weight of glory; While we look not at the things which are seen, but at the things which are not seen: for the things which are seen are temporal; but the things which are not seen are eternal.

Second Corinthians 4:17-18

After reading the verse, I felt as though I could hear Bruce read the words to me. Actually, it was the Holy Spirit speaking to me through his letter. It was as though the Spirit was letting me know that Bruce wanted to tell me, "Mom, get up and go on.

This is a light affliction compared with the eternal glory, and we will all be together soon anyway."

The June after Bruce went to heaven, we were at the hospital with his wife as she gave birth to a beautiful baby girl. The devil tried to kill the baby at birth. The umbilical cord was wrapped around her neck three times with four knots in it. The medical staff told us that if the baby hadn't come early and fast she would have died. She swallowed some amniotic fluid so she had to be flown to a hospital a few hours away. The hospital kept her for five days. God saved her!

In December 1990, our granddaughter's mother remarried, and in September of 1991 she had a new brother. In October 1996, a new sister came and another brother in July 1998, and yet another brother came in August 2001. We have had the joy of keeping all of them many times, except for the youngest.

Our oldest daughter graduated from Southwestern Assembly of God College in 1990, and in December of 1991 she married a wonderful, handsome Christian man. They had a son in February 1993 and a daughter in November 1997.

Our second daughter graduated from Oral Roberts University. She married a wonderful, handsome Christian man in May 1994, and she is a nurse.

Our youngest daughter is also a graduate of Oral Roberts University, and she also married a wonderful, handsome Christian young man in June 1997. They all have continued to maintain excellent grades and their stand for Jesus Christ.

We are so thankful. Psalm 124 teaches that if it were not for the Lord, our enemy would swallow us up. Whatever you may be going through, if you are willing to put your trust in God and stay in His Word in fellowship with him, He will make your situations work toward a good ending and He will bring you through them victoriously.

When thou passest through the waters, I will be with thee; and through the rivers, they shall not overflow thee: when thou walkest through the fire, thou shalt not be burned; neither shall the flame kindle upon thee.

Isaiah 43:2

CHAPTER SIX

CHOOSE TO LIVE

During the entire process with Bruce there were many more instances of God's protection and provision that I didn't tell about.

> *I waited patiently for the LORD; and he inclined unto me, and heard my cry. He brought me up also out of an horrible pit, out of the miry clay, and set my feet upon a rock, and established my goings. And he hath put a new song in my mouth, even praise unto our God: many shall see it, and fear, and shall trust in the LORD. Blessed is that man that maketh the LORD his trust, and respecteth not the proud, nor such as turn aside to lies. Many, O LORD my God, are thy wonderful works which thou hast done, and thy thoughts which are to us-ward: they cannot be reckoned up in order unto thee:*

if I would declare and speak of them, they are more than can be numbered.

Psalm 40:1-5

Nevertheless the LORD thy God would not hearken unto Balaam; but the LORD thy God turned the curse into a blessing unto thee, because the LORD thy God loved thee.

Deuteronomy 23:5

I want to talk to you about abusive spirits because I believe this is a real key. After I was married, I was happy, but at the same time sadness seemed to follow me. My husband and I had both been saved and filled with the Holy Spirit, and we were blessed in so many ways. We even saw many victories, many more than I could ever tell you, but a dark cloud was still hanging over me. My pastor, and other preachers too, told me this.

I wanted to be set free, so I asked God to show me what it was and to liberate me from it. As time passed, I have come to understand that the bondage was the result of generational curses, which were given to me on the day of my birth. I have learned how to be freed from these curses. It comes through the blood of Jesus and through supernatural godly forgiveness. Only in this way can the root of the curse be healed.

Do not glorify the problem. Remember to forgive, and then get on with life. For some people, this may take time. The devil might try to bring thoughts of unforgiveness to you over and over again, but you just have to continue to forgive and to keep the hurt cleansed by the blood of Jesus. By an act of your will you have to choose to forgive, and then you need to ask the Father to help you with your feelings.

Does this mean that we would trust the person who abused us to care for our children or grandchildren? No, we would not unless we were certain through the Holy Spirit that the person is totally changed by the power of God.

*He that hath no rule over his own spirit is like
a city that is broken down, and without walls.*
Proverbs 25:28

When an abusive spirit would try to attach itself to you, people with unregenerated spirits may reach out to the abusive spirit that torments you and be ugly to you or try to violate you. Until that unregenerated person's spirit is conformed to the leading of the Holy Spirit the danger will exist. The devil wants to scar you for life so that you won't do anything for God. But you can cover yourself with the blood of Jesus and the Word of God. (See Isaiah 54:17 and Psalm 91.)

Also, in some cases, it may be necessary for you to forgive the person who allowed the abuse to happen. For instance, if a father was abusing a child and the mother allowed it to go on, the abused person might blame the mother, but in these cases the abused person must forgive.

The devil will tell you that you are ugly, worthless, and stupid, but this isn't the truth. You are a beautiful person and of great worth in Christ Jesus. Jesus paid a very high price for you. You have the mind of Christ.

There is a good possibility that if you were abused, your parents also were abused. Godly, Spirit-filled Christians are destroyed because they do not know how to break the power of the devil over their lives and over the lives of their children.

You must be specific with the devil. Declare that the blood of the Lamb delivers you. Millions have been abused, and most of them have been silent. Many times, young ladies who have been abused have reproductive problems and are unable to have children. Their endometriosis doesn't come from physical harm, but from the curse. Also, many who have been abused have trouble with overeating, bulimia, anorexia, spirits of suicide, depression, and discouragement.

I do not mean to imply that everyone who has struggled with these problems has been abused. There are many who have had trouble in their marriages or in their sex lives because of the physical or emotional trauma that has been inflicted on them.

Some people experience a shutdown of their bodies, and they say they won't have anything to do with the area in which they were traumatized. I suffered problems of this nature in the early part of my marriage, but through prayer God has set me free. He will do the same for you.

Many people feel sorry for themselves because they have gone through much tribulation, but feeling sorry for yourself doesn't improve the situation. Feeling sorry for yourself will cause you to slide deeper into depression. When you glorify the problem, you are making a friend of the curse.

Choose to live and to speak the things that God says! When we speak negatively concerning ourselves, we kill our own faith, and without faith we cannot be healed. Until you are healed of the emotional scar that was caused by the curse of abuse, you will not be healed permanently.

The devil will use spirits of overeating, anorexia, and bulimia, for example, or cause you to suffer from spirits of suicide. The evil one will try to make you overeat or try to make you starve yourself to death. Take charge and command Satan to depart from you, your children, and your grandchildren in Jesus' name, because the blood of Jesus broke the curse! You will never go forward as long as you hang on to the past.

CHAPTER SEVEN

BIRTH GIFTS — WHAT ARE THEY?

[He] *gave himself for us, that he might re-deem us from all iniquity, and purify unto himself a peculiar people, zealous of good works.* Titus 2:14

For all have sinned, and come short of the glory of God. Romans 3:23

And God blessed them, and God said unto them, Be fruitful, and multiply, and replen-ish the earth, and subdue it: and have domin-ion over the fish of the sea, and over the fowl of the air, and over every living thing that moveth upon the earth.
And God said, Behold, I have given you every herb bearing seed, which is upon the face of

all the earth, and every tree, in the which is the fruit of a tree yielding seed; to you it shall be for meat.   Genesis 1:28-29

Adam and Eve had the blessings of God. They had abundant blessing. They lacked nothing, and they had love, joy, peace, health, and fellowship with the Father God, but because of their transgression they lost their blessings for themselves and for the entire world. Genesis 3:6-19 teaches that a curse came upon them, and therefore all are born into sin. Jesus, however, bore our sins.

But he was wounded for our transgressions [sins], he was bruised for our iniquities.
                    Isaiah 53:5

Jesus bore more than our sins. He also bore our iniquities. Understanding the meaning of the word *iniquities* is important. Iniquities are deep-rooted sins, sins practiced until they become wickedness or an uncontrollable desire. Iniquities, then, are the curses that have been given to the descendants of Adam as birthday gifts — those sins which are passed from one generation to the next.

There are generational curses. As defined, one iniquity that may be passed from one generation to the next is uncontrollable desire to sin in a certain area. This iniquity of insatiable desire increases in strength from one generation to the next.

> *As the bird by wandering, as the swallow by flying, so the curse causeless shall not come.*
> Proverbs 26:2

Solomon is saying that there is always a cause for the curse.

All of us were born into a world under the curse, but our sins, or the sins of our parents or grandparents, may compound with each generation.

> *I the LORD thy God am a jealous God, visiting the iniquity of the fathers upon the children unto the third and fourth generation of them that hate me.*
> Exodus 20:5

Family iniquities start with one person's choice to sin or overindulge in an area over and over again without repenting. It becomes iniquity, and if not cleansed, it will become worse with each generation. An example of this is Sodom and Gomorrah. God had to destroy those cities because of the accumulation of iniquity. Other than Lot and his family, the inhabitants of these cities were totally corrupt. God had to destroy them. In Deuteronomy 20:16-17, God told Israel to destroy the Canaanites utterly, because they were totally corrupt. In Joshua 7:24-26, Achan and his family were stoned and burned to keep sin from becoming iniquity. Jeremiah wrote: *Our fathers have sinned, and are not; and we have borne their iniquities* (Lamentation 5:7).

Your grandfather may be dead, but you may still bear the same sinful tendencies. If your great grandfather was an alcoholic or if your mother was a thief or your grandfather was a child abuser, it could affect you, your children, and your grandchildren. You could end up an alcoholic, or your child could become a thief.

Everybody recognizes this curse. If you go to a doctor, he or she may ask your family medical history. Did your parents or grandparents have arthritis, heart trouble, or diabetes? The doctor is asking because you could have a genetic predisposition to a certain disease.

Sometimes curses, whether sin or sickness, will skip a generation or even two. It is true that sin becomes iniquity and is rooted deeper with each passing generation, but there are also examples of people, even those who aren't Christians, who make a decision to abandon a certain sin and do so with success. Each individual does have the power of decision to lay aside a certain sin in his or her own life, but the iniquity can still be carried to the next generation or a later generation if it is not broken by the power of Christ.

Someone whose family has been bound by to-bacco for generations and who suddenly decides that tobacco will not have a place in his or her life, and does not want to give that example to his or her children, can make the decision to abandon tobacco and then make ongoing decisions to support the initial decision.

So sin's root does grow deeper from generation to generation, but an individual can break from it and yet still pass the iniquity to the next generation. Sin is individual choice, but choosing against it becomes more difficult as iniquity increases through generations. Though an individual can make personal decisions to break the power of a certain sin, sin's power is only totally broken by the One who broke every generational curse. We can do the same if we choose to allow His complete work in us and accept His complete work for us.

You may never have used drugs yet have a son who does and wonder why. With each generation, sin is rooted deeper and deeper, unless it is stopped by the blood of Jesus. As this process continues, it will open the door for more sin to come into one's life. For example, a person could become addicted to pornography, and this could lead to rape or murder. Grief could lead to unforgiveness, deep depression, or suicide.

The curse of substance abuse opens the door to the curse of lying and deception. Many substance abusers shut their eyes to their own wrongdoing, not taking the responsibility for their actions. They do not want to deal with correction or penalty, so they lie about their crime, always blaming others for their problems. Sometimes they continue to blame others even after the substance abuse stops.

Many people must deal with negative "gifts," or generational curses that they have inherited. Trials come to everyone, but when we feel sorry for ourselves because we have suffered so much, we make ourselves friends of the curse. This opens the door so that Satan can bring more curses.

Resist the devil, and he will flee from you.
James 4:7

Many people are blind. They do not realize that they are making friends with a curse!

It has happened that a person loses a loved one and receives much love and attention at the time of the funeral. This person starts liking attention so much that the individual begins to look for it constantly. The person begins talking about his or her loss and personal problems. In so doing, a spirit of grief, which is a curse, may come upon this person, along with deep depression and even suicidal thoughts. It may take years to come out of this spirit of grief, or it could eventually kill the afflicted individual if the curse isn't canceled by the blood of Jesus. However, there is a normal grief process and I'm not talking about that. My concern is grief that never ends and persists all the time.

My mother experienced this with the death of our son. It didn't kill her, but it almost did. Grief and guilt can consume you and may be fatal if it is allowed to continue. My mother was a wonderful Christian woman, and a real intercessor. She read her Bible faithfully and was always a strong Christian, but in some way she blamed herself for Bruce's death (which was a lie from the pit of hell).

My mother stopped eating. She looked like a walking skeleton. For more than seven years she sunk deeper and deeper into depression, and everybody she met knew of her great loss within five minutes after she met them. I am not saying you shouldn't share your grief with anyone, but it shouldn't consume your every thought.

She stopped praying and reading her Bible, she never wanted to go anywhere, and finally she wanted to sleep all the time as an escape. In the beginning she was bitter against God. She felt as though He should have stopped the accident from happening.

She didn't understand the choices Bruce made, which led to his death. He made the choice to walk in the curse.

I call heaven and earth to record this day against you, that I have set before you life and death, blessing and cursing: therefore choose life, that both thou and thy seed may live: that thou mayest love the LORD thy God, and that thou mayest obey his voice, and that thou mayest cleave unto him: for he is thy life, and the length of thy days: that thou mayest dwell in the land which the LORD sware unto thy fathers, to Abraham, to Isaac, and to Jacob, to give them.   Deuteronomy 30:19-20

The Lord said to choose life. The things Bruce chose brought death. He chose sex, drinking, and other sins. He knew what he was doing was wrong, but he didn't understand the curse and he didn't understand that he could do something to break it. My mother didn't understand this either. The Bible says in Hosea 4:6 that we are *destroyed for lack of knowledge.*

For more than seven years my mother walked in the shadow of death, but finally, little by little, she began to get better and she became stronger. She returned to church and read her Bible. The Word of God really brought life to her.

My mother finally received her deliverance. She was completely healed emotionally, and her body did gain strength, though she still had some effects in her body from the years of grieving. Proverbs 4:22 teaches that the Word is life to us and health to all our flesh. She began to participate in her inheritance in Christ Jesus.

The Holy Spirit is our Comforter, and He will lift our grief if we let him. Isaiah 53:5 says that *"with His stripes we are healed."* Praise God! My mother had nearly reached the grave, and she came back a beautiful person in spirit and soul, just as she had been.

People have to want deliverance; others cannot force it on them. We cannot afford bitterness and unforgiveness; we must forgive. Forgiveness is a choice. Forgiveness means giving up on revenge. I am not saying that if someone is beating you up all the time, you should stay in such a situation. I am just saying that you are to forgive. You cannot change what has already happened, but you can take steps to prevent the abuse from happening again.

I was having a hard time forgiving someone for something that was said one time, and as I prayed about it I chose to forgive but was still having trouble with my own feelings. The Lord said to me to just pretend it had never been said. If it had never been spoken, I wouldn't have had a hard time walking in love. So the pretending made it easy. I just played like it never happened. I'm not saying you should pretend you weren't abused, or anything like that. This applied in my particular situation but may not with yours. We do have to face those kinds of hurts or abuses, forgive, and go on with our lives. We should always seek the Lord's instruction in these matters.

We are a spirit, we have a soul, and we live in a body. Our spirit's voice is our conscience, our soul's is our intellect, and our body's is our feelings. When we ask Jesus into our heart, the Holy Spirit indwells our spirit. Whether or not you are a Christian, your personal spirit will try to guide you based on the morals you have been taught. When you become a Christian by asking Jesus into your heart, you are born again and made brand new. The Holy Spirit indwells your spirit and becomes the voice of your conscience, teaching you right from wrong.

Therefore if any man be in Christ, he is a new creature: old things are passed away; behold, all things are become new.
Second Corinthians 5:17

When you get saved, you may not see change in your body immediately. Your soul (mind) changes as you renew it by meditating on the Word over and over again until the Word becomes a part of you. You should never stop renewing your mind in the Word of God. Paul said,

But I keep under my body, and bring it into subjection: lest that by any means, when I have preached to others, I myself should be a castaway. First Corinthians 9:27

We have to take the responsibility of bringing our bodies into subjection. If you have not asked Jesus into your heart, you can, even this very moment, by believing:

That if thou shalt confess with thy mouth the Lord Jesus, and shalt believe in thine heart that God hath raised him from the dead, thou shalt be saved. For with the heart man believeth unto righteousness; and with the mouth confession is made unto salvation.

Romans 10:9-10

But for us also, to whom it shall be imputed, if we believe on him that raised up Jesus our Lord from the dead; who was delivered for our offences, and was raised again for our justification. Romans 4:24-25

For God so loved the world, that he gave his only begotten Son, that whosoever believeth in him should not perish, but have everlasting life.

John 3:16

If you believe, then pray this prayer in your heart:

Heavenly Father, I come to You now, I am a sinner, but I choose to turn away from my sin. I ask You to cleanse me from all unrighteousness. Thank You that the blood of Jesus cleanses me. I believe Jesus died for me. His blood took away my sins. I also believe that He rose again from the dead so that I might be justified, and He has made me righteous through faith in Him. I ask Jesus Christ to be my Savior and Lord over all my life.

Jesus, I choose to follow You, and I ask that You fill me with the power of the Holy Spirit. I declare that I am a born-again child of God, free from sin and full of the righteousness of God. I am saved in Jesus' name, the name above every name. Amen.

There is therefore now no condemnation to them which are in Christ Jesus, who walk not after the flesh, but after the Spirit. For the law of the Spirit of life in Christ Jesus hath made me free from the law of sin and death.

Romans 8:1-2

If we do not know the blood covenant and the written covenant (the Word of God), we cannot walk in them. We must read the Word and find out what our covenant says.

> *Ye are of God, little children, and have overcome them: because greater is he that is in you, than he that is in the world.*   First John 4:4

So, we can stand against the devil, not in our own strength but in God's strength! We can speak out the Word of God and obey it, and the devil must flee.

> *Submit yourselves therefore to God. Resist the devil, and he will flee from you.*   James 4:7

Remember that no matter what you are facing, no matter how big the problem is, *your God* is a lot bigger!

You must choose, through Jesus Christ, to be victorious in your attitude in spite of your situation. Making this choice is the first step to deliverance. Once you have Jesus in your heart, continue to believe and speak out what the Word says. Proclaim that you are redeemed from the curse:

> *Christ hath redeemed us from the curse of the law, being made a curse for us: for it is written, Cursed is every one that hangeth on a tree.*   Galatians 3:13

You must know that you are valuable and precious to Father God. Jesus paid a very high price to redeem you. You are priceless. You are invaluable. You must learn to love yourself, before you can expect others to love you.

> *Choose life, that both thou and thy seed may live.* Deuteronomy 30:19

God wants you to have abundant life. He gives the victory through His name, His blood, and His Word. The choice to receive this abundant life is yours.

Psalm 8:5 explains that God has placed a crown of glory and honor upon our heads. He has given us charge over everything (Ephesians 1:19-23). He has made it so that everything is under the authority of the name of Jesus Christ (Philippians 2:9-10), and through His blood any curse we have inherited is canceled (Galatians 3:13).

God will not break His covenant, because He cannot lie and the covenant is based on the blood of His Son and on faith in His name. He has given us His strength for our weakness.

> *My grace is sufficient for thee: for my strength is made perfect in weakness.* Second Corinthians 12:9

We are empowered by His Spirit with supernatural ability to overcome, and we are empowered with "the blessing." Jesus bore every curse, including heart problems, kidney problems, cancer, all sickness, poverty, emotional problems — in short, every need — on the cross. His death, burial and resurrection made a completed work, covering all the needs of all mankind.

That's why that when we get into the glory (the presence of God), we are changed from glory to glory, and we walk each day in greater depth in God, reaching new heights in Him, walking more fully in His provision and in His grace, His enabling power.

> *My sheep hear my voice, and I know them,*
> *and they follow me.* John 10:27

He communicates Spirit to spirit.

> *I will never leave thee, nor forsake thee.*
> Hebrews 13:5

God does not leave us. However, one can choose sin and step out from under the covering of God. God does not leave us, but we can leave His presence. Sin separates us from God.

> *If we confess our sins, he is faithful and just to*
> *forgive us our sins, and to cleanse us from all*
> *unrighteousness.* First John 1:9

77

The blood of Jesus brings us back into the blessing. By our asking for forgiveness the blood cleanseth us, but we must know and speak the Word in order to walk in the blessings. God loves you so much that He sent His Son to die for you, but He will not make you walk in His blessing. He gives you the choice.

The devil cannot make you serve him, but he will try. Remember, he is a defeated foe. Jesus defeated Satan for us. You were dead in sins, and your sinful desires were not yet cut away. Then He gave you a share in the very life of Christ, for He forgave all your sins and blotted out the charges against you.

He took this list of sins and destroyed it by nailing it to Christ's cross. In this way God took away Satan's power to accuse you of sin, and God openly displayed to the whole world Christ's triumph at the cross where your sins were all taken away. Colossians 2:14-15 (TLB)

Chapter Eight

The Promise Is for You

God wants to show us the hidden causes of failures and defeat in our lives and in our families. As we discover the truth of God's Word and apply it to our lives, new birth gifts of blessing replace the birth gifts of curses in our lives and in our families. Because Jesus was bruised for our iniquities, it is possible for us to receive the blessing instead of cursing.

I wish to make one thing very clear again. Sinning once doesn't mean that someone is under a curse. Sinning once in a certain area will make it easier to sin in that area again. But it is the continuing in a particular sin over and over that makes a sin an inquity, and this is what brings a curse to the sinner and to others after him or her.

There are many curses that we can fall into. Poverty is a curse. This curse is seen both in believers and in nonbelievers, and it is often passed from one generation to another. Poverty breeds crime, carelessness, shame, and immorality.

Anti-Semitism (hatred or resentment of Jews) brings with it a curse of insufficiency. God said to Abraham:

> *And I will bless them that bless thee, and curse him that curseth thee: and in thee shall all families of the earth be blessed.*
>
> Genesis 12:3

Blessing can be shut off by bitterness, complaining, gossiping, unforgiveness, and by being prejudiced. Gossip is a curse that eats like a cancer. Do not speak against your employer. Judge not so you will not be judged, for when we judge others, we bring judgment on ourselves. Respect those in authority, not judging them. In every job, keep in mind that the Lord is your real boss, so do your work unto Him.

> *And whatsoever ye do, do it heartily, as to the Lord, and not unto men.* Colossians 3:23

When we are judging our boss, we are not doing our work as unto the Lord. It is important to watch what we speak over fellow employees, over our fellow members in the church, over the Body of Christ, and especially over our family.

It is easy to open up to a critical spirit that can bring a curse. By being critical and judgmental we step out from under God's blessings, and we then open ourselves to the enemy.

For he that eateth and drinketh unworthily, eateth and drinketh damnation to himself, not discerning the Lord's body. For this cause many are weak and sickly among you, and many sleep. For if we would judge ourselves, we should not be judged.
First Corinthians 11:29-31

Speaking against your pastors brings a curse. Therefore, guard your tongue. Don't bite the hand that feeds you.

Touch not mine anointed, and do my prophets no harm.
First Chronicles 16:22 and Psalm 105:15

Numbers 12:1-15 tells about when Miriam and Aaron spoke against Moses and Miriam was afflicted with the curse of leprosy. Second Kings 2:23-24 tells of the children who mocked Elisha and the curse of the two bears that ripped up the forty-two children.

We need to teach our children to respect God's anointed. Disobedience can also bring a curse.

Children need to obey their parents and respect them so that blessing comes, rather than a curse.

Children, obey your parents in the Lord: for this is right. Honour thy father and mother; which is the first commandment with promise; that it may be well with thee, and thou mayest live long on the earth.

Ephesians 6:1-3

The purpose for which we have been born is safeguarded by our obedience to God. It is also manifest as we obey Him. However, God also requires us to obey parents and all who have authority over us, in accordance with the Word. If you are married and gone from home you should still respect your parents, but you cannot allow them to control your life at that point, for if you do, that may also bring a curse.

He that troubleth his own house shall inherit the wind: and the fool shall be servant to the wise of heart.

Proverbs 11:29

In this case, the troubling could be from family control and manipulation. It could be ignoring each other. It could be violence, abuse, hate, or even something so apparently innocent as nagging.

Greed could also be trouble for your house, according to Proverbs 15:27. If pursuing wealth is more important than seeking first the Kingdom of God, then there is idolatry, and this can bring a curse. However, believing for prosperity to further the Kingdom of God is not greed. Such prosperity is good and right.

> *Thou shalt have none other gods before me. Thou shalt not make thee any graven image, or any likeness of any thing that is in heaven above, or that is in the earth beneath, or that is in the waters beneath the earth: thou shalt not bow down thyself unto them, nor serve them: for I the LORD thy God am a jealous God, visiting the iniquity of the fathers upon the children unto the third and fourth generation of them that hate me.*
>
> Deuteronomy 5:7-9

God does not want other gods in our homes. God will not share the throne of your heart with other gods, nor will He share His presence in your home with other gods. Be watchful of what you bring into your home. Also, people sometimes pick up things that are related to the worship of other gods. This happens especially with items from other countries. It is good to go share the Gospel in a foreign country, being led there by the Holy Spirit, but take care not to bring home objects that have been devoted to the worship of pagan gods or that have Satanic connection.

Televison can become a god if you spend a lot of time watching it and give God only five or ten minutes. In such a case, TV is a god. God will not tolerate sin, so if you want God in your life and house, sin has to go. Obedience brings blessing. Disobedience robs us of the ability to prosper. It cuts our productivity and our means of survival, and it steals our health.

So, whatever sin is in our life, we must repent and remove it because that separates us from God. We have to clean our house of sinful things in the natural as well as in the spiritual. We must stay filled with the Holy Spirit, keep the Word of God in us, and spend time in the presence of our Father God so that we can spiritually discern right from wrong. According to the Bible, we should get rid of anything that deals with the occult, evil spirits, or false doctrines. There may be other things that the Holy Spirit may lead you to clean out of your home.

Another curse many fall into is fear. Fear can become a real stronghold if we allow it to gain a foothold in our lives.

For God hath not given us the spirit of fear; but of power, and of love, and of a sound mind.
Second Timothy 1:7

Tithing is another area where we may choose to walk in blessing or to walk in the curse.

Will a man rob God? Yet ye have robbed me. But ye say, Wherein have we robbed thee? In tithes and offerings. Ye are cursed with a curse: for ye have robbed me, even this whole nation. Bring ye all the tithes into the storehouse, that there may be meat in mine house, and prove me now herewith, saith the LORD of hosts, if I will not open you the windows of heaven, and pour you out a blessing, that there shall not be room enough to receive it.
Malachi 3:8-10

Violence also opens the door to a curse. People who commit violence, who enjoy watching violence, or who condone violence are under a curse. Keep violence out of your home and away from your children and grandchildren.

Sexual sins such as adultery, fornication, lesbianism, homosexuality, sexual abuse, incest, rape, pornography, and pedophilia seem to bring one of the very worst curses, and its ill effects are devastating. God is a merciful God, but He will not live with sin. He is looking for people who will hunger and thirst after Him.

Who will walk in His holiness? A curse such as pornography can affect the whole family. It can bring fear, nightmares, shame, an inferiority complex, and much more.

As you can see, there are many generational curses. When you allow them into your home, you soon see that the atmosphere in which you live destroys life, and it does not bring renewal. You soon find yourself in a sterile, lifeless house that is dominated by anger, strife, sorrow, and death.

Instead of the curse, we can choose the blood of Jesus. He is the way, the truth, and the life. Fill your home with an atmosphere of peace, joy, laughter, respect, and renewal. Choose life! When the Holy Spirit controls our lives, He will produce this kind of fruit in us: love joy, peace, patience, kindness, goodness, faithfulness, gentleness, and self-control, according to Galatians 5: 22, 23 (TLB). When we fill our hearts with faith instead of fear, good things will come out of our mouths.

So then faith cometh by hearing, and hearing by the word of God. Romans 10:17

Genesis 1:26 teaches that we are made in His image, and Romans 8:17 teaches that we are joint heirs with Jesus Christ.

You will not overcome curses by your own strength. It can only be done with the blood of the Lord Jesus Christ, through God's power. The price has already been paid; the gift has already been given. You do not have to become good enough for it or earn it. You only need to receive it and walk in it.

Thou wilt shew me the path of life: in thy presence is fulness of joy; at thy right hand there are pleasures for evermore.

Psalm 16:11

The only way to receive blessing gifts is to know Jesus Christ as your Lord and Savior. When you do, His blood reverses the curse and changes it to blessing. You may say, "Well, I know someone who has accepted the Lord, and he still walks in the curse." The Bible explains why this sometimes occurs.

My people are destroyed for lack of knowledge: because thou hast rejected knowledge, I will also reject thee, that thou shalt be no priest to me: seeing thou hast forgotten the law of thy God, I will also forget thy children.

Hosea 4:6

We are kings and priests, redeemed by the blood of the Lamb, Jesus Christ, but if we do not know what is ours in Christ, the devil will come and destroy us. You do not have to accept the gifts that are curses that were given to you on your day of birth. Those gifts of curses were sent from Satan. Now, with Christ, you can mark them for return to sender.

Do not accept the gifts of abuse, depression, sickness, poverty, fear, worry, or whatever Satan may be trying to put on you. These gifts need not be your "birth day" gifts. Tell Satan that he has the wrong address! Tell him that you aren't in his family anymore and that by the blood of Jesus, the curse has been broken. Tell him that you are in Jesus' family now.

Jesus bore the curse for us so that we don't have to be cursed. He has called us out of darkness and brought us into His marvelous light, according to First Peter 2:9. He has brought us out of fear, worry, doubt, insecurity, sickness, poverty, and much, much more. He has brought us into peace, joy, faith, love, security, healing, health, abundance, and much, much, much more! Freedom is ours as long as we choose truth, stand firm in the strength of the Lord — in His Word — and claim the power in the blood of Jesus Christ. Know that at the name of Jesus every curse must bow.

I call heaven and earth to record this day against you, that I have set before you life and

death, blessing and cursing: therefore choose
life, that both thou and thy seed may live.
                                    Deuteronomy 30:19

You will never perfect what you do not practice. Practice the Word, and eliminate weakness in your life. You must come to a point of decision where you refuse to walk in the curse anymore and you reach a point of receiving what Jesus Christ did for you through His death, burial, and resurrection. Presenting His blood to the Father, He became our mercy seat. Be a follower of Jesus. Walk as He walked.

My son, attend to my words; incline thine ear
unto my sayings. Let them not depart from
thine eyes; keep them in the midst of thine
heart. For they are life unto those that find
them, and health to all their flesh.
Keep thy heart with all diligence; for out of it
are the issues of life.   Proverbs 4:20-23

Trust in the LORD with all thine heart; and
lean not unto thine own understanding. In
all thy ways acknowledge him, and he shall
direct thy paths.   Proverbs 3:5-6

Unless the curse is broken by the blood of Jesus, it will go on from generation to generation without regard for culture, training, or environment.

For the mystery of iniquity doth already work: only he who now letteth will let, until he be taken out of the way.

Second Thessalonians 2:7

It may not have started with you, but someone in your parentage repeatedly sinned in a certain area until it became an iniquity (a deep rooted sin, a weakness, or a curse). The only way it can be stopped is by confessing sin and accepting what the blood of Jesus has done.

If we confess our sins, he is faithful and just to forgive us our sins, and to cleanse us from all unrighteousness. First John 1:9

Deuteronomy 28:1-14 lists the blessings. A few of them are blessings in the city, blessings in the field, many children, ample crops, large flocks and herds, blessings of fruit and bread, blessings when you come in, and blessings when you go out. Verse 14 teaches that blessing depends on obedience, and it also teaches that you must never worship other gods. Deuteronomy 7:25-26 tells how false gods will keep a person from the blessing.

Renounce any involvement you have, or have had, with the occult. Exodus 20:3-5 teaches not to have any other gods before Him or to have or make any graven images. The rest of Deuteronomy 28 lists the curses, such as curses in the city and curses in the fields. There are curses on fruit and bread, and there is the curse of the barren womb. Curses are pronounced upon the crops and upon the fertility of the cattle and the flocks. There are curses on coming in and curses on going out.

However, we know that:

> *Christ hath redeemed us from the curse of the law, being made a curse for us: for it is written, Cursed is every one that hangeth on a tree.*
> Galatians 3:13

> *Thou hast forgiven the iniquity of thy people, thou hast covered all their sin. Selah.*
> Psalm 85:2

If you are not experiencing freedom in your daily life, it may be because you did not realize who you are in Jesus Christ (the Anointed One) and in His anointing. Finding out who you are in Christ and what you have in Him is an important key to walking in the blessing, free from the curse. There are many scriptures that speak of who we are and what we have "in Christ." Here are a few:

91

For he hath made him to be sin for us, who knew no sin; that we might be made the righteousness of God in him.
Second Corinthians 5:21

Your old evil desires were nailed to the cross with him; that part of you that loves to sin was crushed and fatally wounded, so that your sin-loving body is no longer under sin's control, no longer needs to be slave to sin.
Romans 6:6 (TLB)

Wherefore if ye be dead with Christ from the rudiments of the world, why, as though living in the world, are ye subject to ordinances?
Colossians 2:20

For ye are dead, and your life is hid with Christ in God.
Colossians 3:3

For in that he died, he died unto sin once: but in that he liveth, he liveth unto God. Likewise reckon ye also yourselves to be dead indeed unto sin, but alive unto God through Jesus Christ our Lord.
Romans 6: 10-11

If we sow forgiveness, we will reap forgiveness. As we forgive, the Word will set us free and give life to those areas that are dead because of sin. The Holy Spirit will purge you with the blood of Jesus, apply healing, and make you whole. He shines light on those things you need to change, and brings healing oil to the deep bruises of your heart. The blood of Jesus will cleanse you and your family.

It is up to you to choose to break the pattern of sin. You can walk in the healing of those trespasses committed against you and in the forgiveness of those you committed. There isn't any reason to stay bound any longer. The choice is yours. It is up to you to choose to break the sinful pattern of your past by the name of Jesus and by the blood of the Lamb, thus turning family curses and the gifts of curses given to you at birth into the blessing of new gifts for your day of birth that will last a thousand generations.

Know therefore that the LORD thy God, he is God, the faithful God, which keepeth covenant and mercy with them that love him and keep his commandments to a thousand generations. Deuteronomy 7:9

This promise is for you and for the generations to come after you.

Once you were under God's curse, doomed forever for your sins. You went along with the crowd and were just like all the others, full of sin, obeying Satan, the mighty prince of the power of the air, who is at work right now in the hearts of those who are against the Lord. All of us used to be just as they are, our lives expressing the evil within us, doing every wicked thing that our passions or our evil thoughts might lead us into. We started out bad, being born with evil natures, and were under God's anger just like everyone else.

But God is so rich in mercy; he loved us so much that even though we were spiritually dead and doomed by our sins, he gave us back our lives again when he raised Christ from the dead — only by his undeserved favor have we ever been saved — and lifted us up from the grave into glory along with Christ, where we sit with him in the heavenly realms — all because of what Christ Jesus did. And now God can always point to us as examples of how very, very rich his kindness is, as shown in all he has done for us through Jesus Christ.

Because of His kindness you have been saved through trusting Christ. And even trusting is not of yourselves; it too is a gift from God. Sal-

vation is not a reward for the good we have done, so none of us can take any credit for it. It is God himself who has made us what we are and given us new lives from Christ Jesus, and long ages ago he planned that we should spend these lives in helping others.

Ephesians 2:1-10 (TLB)

God is not the originator of sickness and disease.

Every good gift and every perfect gift is from above, and cometh down from the Father of lights, with whom is no variableness, neither shadow of turning.   James 1:17

Jesus bore sickness for us so that we would not have to walk under that curse of sickness and by His stripes we have been healed (see First Peter 2:24).

And Jesus knew their thoughts, and said unto them, Every kingdom divided against itself is brought to desolation; and every city or house divided against itself shall not stand.

Matthew 12:25

If sickness was of God, He would not have sent Jesus to bear it for us.

[He] forgiveth all thine iniquities; [he] healeth all thy diseases. Psalm 103:3

When your life and your house have been cleansed by Jesus' blood, don't allow sin to return. Familiar spirits (those that are familiar with you and your family) will seek to come back and to bring more evil spirits with them.

And when he is come, he findeth it empty, swept, and garnished. Then goeth he, and taketh with himself seven other spirits more wicked than himself, and they enter in and dwell there: and the last state of that man is worse than the first. Matthew 12:44-45

With all of this in mind, continue to make a choice to walk in the blessing!

CHAPTER NINE

YOUR GIFTS

Were you given a rich heritage of knowing who you are in Jesus Christ? Do you know what you have in Him? Do you understand what He purchased for you through His death, burial, resurrection, and ascension to the right hand of the Most High God? Were you taught when you were growing up that Jesus' blood, which was shed on the cross of Calvary, was taken to the mercy seat of Heaven to cover your sins and to reverse and destroy every generational curse so that the gifts given you at birth all become blessings?

Maybe you were born into a family with alcoholic parents who ended up in prison. Maybe every evil and mean thing imaginable has been given to you. If so, don't be dismayed. God can turn it around through the blood of Jesus Christ.

Perhaps you were born somewhere in between the extremes of evil and good. Are you a Christian who still seems to be struggling with certain weaknesses in your life? You see the blessings of healing, health, safety, soundness, provision, preservation, deliverance, love, joy, peace, acceptance, and security, but things in your life keep you from walking in them consistently. There is hope for you also. You must never stop walking in the blessings that have been promised to you through Jesus Christ, our Lord and Savior.

Whatever gifts you were given at birth from your natural parents really don't matter if you accept what Jesus Christ has done for you. Once you are born again you belong to God's family. Through Jesus' blood and His completed work, the curse that was upon you has been broken and reversed and the blessings of the new blood Covenant belong to you. The New Covenant is found in Jesus' promise:

> *I am come that they might have life, and that*
> *they might have it more abundantly.*
>
> John 10:10

The New Covenant means that we can have life with nothing broken, nothing missing, and without lack in any area of our lives.

> *The LORD is my shepherd; I shall not want.*
>
> Psalm 23:1

Sins of the body, the mind, and the human spirit bring the curses.

There are word curses. Through our words we can support the plan of God or aid the plan of Satan. God has a plan for our lives:

> *For I know the thoughts that I think toward you, saith the LORD, thoughts of peace, and not of evil, to give you an expected end.*
> Jeremiah 29:11

Satan also has a plan for us:

> *The thief cometh not, but for to steal, and to kill, and to destroy.* John 10:10

Many people have negative thoughts and speak negative words. When these thoughts come out of their mouths, it is because evil and wrong words have come into their ears and this has filled their hearts (see Matthew 12:34-35). The Lord teaches that whatever is in your heart will come out of your mouth. So guard your heart. Out of it come the issues of life.

> *Death and life are in the power of the tongue.*
> Proverbs 18:21

99

We must watch what we speak over our children. If we say things like "You are so slow," "You're stupid," or "You're clumsy," we are putting them under a curse. A teacher, a pastor, or a person in authority can do this, but we as parents can stop the curse by the blood of the Lamb and the word of our testimony (see Revelation 12:11).

We shape our children's lives by what we speak over them. Speak good things over your children. Say things like "You are so kind," "You are so neat and you always do a good job cleaning your room," and "You get good grades." Praise and affirmation are important.

Speak the Word over them. Say, "You are healed by Jesus' stripes" (see First Peter 2:24), "You're more than a conqueror through Christ" (see Romans 8:37), or "Christ always causes you to triumph" (see Second Corinthians 2:14).

In Isaiah 6:6-7, the angel took a coal off the altar and touched Isaiah's lips so he could speak God's words. His iniquity was taken away, and his sin was purged. Our words are very powerful! We must speak the Word over ourselves and not speak evil, which brings self-imposed curses.

If you have spoken curses and brought them upon yourself, with words such as "My brain just died," "I'm so fat," or "I'll never be good enough for that blessing," then repent and accept the blood of

Jesus to reverse the curse. Revoke what you spoke, and replace it with the Word of God.

> *That the communication of thy faith may become effectual by the acknowledging of every good thing which is in you in Christ Jesus.*
> Philemon 6

> *I can do all things through Christ which strengtheneth me.* Philippians 4:13

> *We have the mind of Christ.*
> First Corinthians 2:16

> *I am fearfully and wonderfully made.*
> Psalm 139:14

> *That ye put off concerning the former conversation the old man, which is corrupt according to the deceitful lusts; and be renewed in the spirit of your mind; and that ye put on the new man, which after God is created in righteousness and true holiness.*
> Ephesians 4:22-24

It is so important that you don't exalt the sin of your children, grandchildren, husband, wife, friend, or of anyone, for that matter. Exalt the Word of God. It will bring victory.

[God shows] *mercy unto thousands of them that love me, and keep my commandments.*
Exodus 20:6

If you don't realize what your true birth gifts are that you have from Christ, it will be easy for you to pass on curses to your children. Many parents do not wish to admit that what they do and say does affect their children, but it does. We can pass on blessing to our children and grandchildren.

[God visits] *the iniquity of the fathers upon the children unto the third and fourth generation of them that hate me.* Exodus 20:5

Your words have been stout against me, saith the LORD. Malachi 3:13

Our words have greater power than we realize. Iniquities become embedded deeply in the mind (the will) until evil controls the person in whom they dwell, and they are then passed down from one generation to the next. Those curses are only broken by the blood of Jesus.

God the Father chose you long ago and knew you would become his children, And the Holy Spirit has been at work in your hearts, cleans-

ing you with the blood of Jesus Christ and making you to please him. May God bless you richly and grant you increasing freedom from all anxiety and fear.

First Peter 1:2 (TLB)

But ye are come...to Jesus the mediator of the new covenant, and to the blood of sprinkling, that speaketh better things than that of Abel.

Hebrews 12:22, 24

The New Covenant is better than the Old Covenant. Through the New Covenant we have been made one with Jesus Christ. In return for our sins He has given us a robe of righteousness, and He has given us His strength in place of our weakness. He has made us so much His own that He has even given us His name and the authority to use it.

And these signs shall follow them that believe; In my name shall they cast out devils.

Mark 16:17

The devil has no right to put curses on us. We must rise up and take our place as covenant partners with the Father God through Jesus.

But now hath he obtained a more excellent ministry, by how much also he is the media-

*tor of a better covenant, which was estab-
lished upon better promises.*   Hebrews 8:6

*Whereof the Holy Ghost also is a witness to
us: for after that he had said before, This is
the covenant that I will make with them after those days, saith the Lord, I will put my
laws into their hearts, and in their minds will
I write them; and their sins and iniquities will
I remember no more. Now where remission
of these is, there is no more offering for sin.*
Hebrews 10:15-18

*Forasmuch as ye know that ye were not re-
deemed with corruptible things, as silver and
gold, from your vain conversation received by
tradition from your fathers; but with the precious blood of Christ, as of a lamb without
blemish and without spot: who verily was
foreordained before the foundation of the
world, but was manifest in these last times for
you.*
*Being born again, not of corruptible seed, but
of incorruptible, by the word of God, which
liveth and abideth for ever.*
First Peter 1:18-20, 23

*But if we walk in the light, as he is in the light,
we have fellowship one with another, and the*

blood of Jesus Christ his Son cleanseth us from all sin.
If we confess our sins, he is faithful and just to forgive us our sins, and to cleanse us from all unrighteousness.

First John 1:7,9

Through the blood of Jesus we have life, and we have life more abundantly (see John 10:10).

Birth gifts that are blessings empower believers to succeed through the power of the Holy Ghost. Birth gifts that are curses debilitate and cause failure.

The blessing of the LORD, it maketh rich, and he addeth no sorrow with it.

Proverbs 10:22

In the Old Testament (see Genesis 17:16; 25:5, 11; 26:12; 27:27; 28:4), Abraham and Sarah, Isaac, and Jacob all walked in the blessing. Joseph also walked in blessing, even when he was in prison. They were clothed with God's righteousness and thus received blessings to succeed.

And all nations shall call you blessed: for ye shall be a delightsome land, saith the LORD of hosts. Malachi 3:12

And it shall come to pass in that day, that his burden shall be taken away from off thy shoulder, and his yoke from off thy neck, and the yoke shall be destroyed because of the anointing. Isaiah 10:27

The blessing — the anointing or the empowerment — will remove burdens, destroy yokes, and remove and destroy curses. God will empower you to do all He has called you to do. God wants to be part of everything you are, everything you do, and everything you say. You are the deciding witness in your life.

I call heaven and earth to record this day against you, that I have set before you life and death, blessing and cursing: therefore choose life, that both thou and thy seed may live. Deuteronomy 30:19

Jesus is the High Priest of the words He anoints that we speak, and He brings them to pass. The Word, which is the truth that we speak, will change the apparent facts that seem to contradict the truth of the Word. Christ has redeemed us from the curse (see Galatians 3:13).

You will never be truly successful as long as you hang on to the past. Jesus came to set us free and keep us free. What God did in Jesus is far greater than what Satan did through Adam.

God made us perfect, but the curse brought defects. When we are reborn, all spiritual defects are taken away from us. God has a plan for each one of us individually.

For I know the thoughts that I think toward you, saith the LORD, thoughts of peace, and not of evil, to give you an expected end.
Jeremiah 29:11

God always sees us in faith. His thoughts toward us are thoughts of peace, and with the best outcome.

For since the beginning of the world men have not heard, nor perceived by the ear, neither hath the eye seen, O God, beside thee, what he hath prepared for him that waiteth for him. Isaiah 64:4

Behold, I will bring it health and cure, and I will cure them, and will reveal unto them the abundance of peace and truth. And I will cause the captivity of Judah and the captivity of Israel to return, and will build them, as at the first. And I will cleanse them from all their iniquity, whereby they have sinned against me; and I will pardon all their iniquities, whereby they have sinned, and whereby they have transgressed against me.

And it shall be to me a name of joy, a praise and an honour before all the nations of the earth, which shall hear all the good that I do unto them: and they shall fear and tremble for all the goodness and for all the prosperity that I procure unto it.   Jeremiah 33:6-9

God blessed us with our heavenly inheritance in Christ Jesus before the foundation of the world and ordained Jesus to see to it that we don't lose it.

But we speak the wisdom of God in a mystery, even the hidden wisdom, which God ordained before the world unto our glory.

Now we have received, not the spirit of the world, but the spirit which is of God; that we might know the things that are freely given to us of God.   First Corinthians 2:7,12

We have godly wisdom by His Spirit:

But we have the mind of Christ.
            First Corinthians 2:16

Blessed be the God and Father of our Lord Jesus Christ, who hath blessed us with all spiritual blessings in heavenly places in Christ: according as he hath chosen us in him before the foundation of the world, that we should be holy and without blame before him in love: having predestinated us unto the adoption of children by Jesus Christ to himself, according to the good pleasure of his will, to the praise of the glory of his grace, wherein he hath made us accepted in the beloved.

Ephesians 1:3-6

Forasmuch as ye know that ye were not redeemed with corruptible things...But with the precious blood of Christ, as of a lamb without blemish and without spot: Who verily was foreordained before the foundation of the world, but was manifest in these last times for you.

First Peter 1:18-20

Before the foundation of the world God reserved great wealth in Christ Jesus for every human being (see Ephesians 1:3,4). This wealth is the blessing, which is His eternal covenant!

For God, who commanded the light to shine out of darkness, hath shined in our hearts, to *give the **light** of the knowledge of the **glory of God in the face of Jesus Christ**. But we have this treasure in earthen vessels, **that the excellency of the power may be of God**, and not of us.* Second Corinthians 4:6-7

Thy face, L<small>ORD</small>, will I seek. Psalm 27:8

As we seek His face we enter His glory. In His glory the blessing "birth day" gifts are that every need is met. God wants us to walk in the blessing, going from glory to glory so that we can be changed into the image of God.

Our hearts must be cleansed first. When we ask Jesus into our hearts, His blood cleanses us. We can ask the Holy Spirit to show us things in our lives that we need to stop or to change. These are the things that may be opening the door to curses and bringing evil into our minds, bodies, and homes.

You may pray and take all of the steps towards freedom, but if you allow your children to play with Pokemon toys, and let them read Harry Potter books, you will open the door of their hearts to much evil, and that can open the door to witchcraft, murder, Satanism, violence, homosexuality, and other evil things. There are so many toys, games, books, songs, movies, and television programs today that are very evil.

Ask the Holy Spirit to show you those things that aren't of God. Don't be deceived. Even though some people say it's a good movie, for instance, you might know from the previews that it is like a monster that would bring evil spirits of fear into your home, so don't open the door to it. What will it bring? A short clip of some dark thing might open a door to nightmares for your children or create a curiosity in them for things they don't recognize as harmful.

Music can be wonderful and can bring the presence of the Lord, but it can also come from the pit of hell and bring the presence of the devil and his evil spirits.

Bruce was given many curses on the day of his birth, but he opened the door to the devil wider with the books, the music, and the games he played with Satan and his dragons (demons) of evil.

Keep thy heart with all diligence; for out of it are the issues of life. Proverbs 4:23

If you put garbage in, you will get garbage coming out. If you bring garbage into your home, garbage will flow out of your home and your life.

Remember, God won't live with sin. He wants us to live holy lives.

Because it is written, Be ye holy; for I am holy.
First Peter 1:16

If we allow garbage in our home, we will soon find that the environment in which we live destroys life instead of renewing it. It is our responsibility to do whatever is necessary to maintain a right relationship with God. Guard your heart and set a watch over your mouth.

Set a watch, O LORD, before my mouth; keep the door of my lips. Psalm 141:3

When you pray and the Holy Spirit checks you on what you are about to say, then don't say it. Speak the Word; speak a blessing instead of a curse. Always renew your mind in the Word of God.

The entrance of thy words giveth light; it giveth understanding unto the simple.
Psalm 119:130

Find a good, Spirit-filled, Word-teaching church, and attend regularly.

Not forsaking the assembling of ourselves together, as the manner of some is; but exhorting one another: and so much the more, as ye see the day approaching. Hebrews 10:25

Pray without ceasing.
First Thessalonians 5:17

Stay in tune with the Holy Spirit. Spend time in His presence. *"In thy presence is fullness of joy"* (Psalm 16:11). *"Rejoice evermore"* (First Thessalonians 5:16). *"Rejoice in the Lord alway, and again I say, Rejoice"* (Philippians 4:4).

Rejoice in the God of our salvation. Choose to be happy. Plead the blood of Jesus in the name of Jesus over yourself and your family. Guard your mind.

Casting down imaginations, and every high thing that exalteth itself against the knowledge of God, and bringing into captivity every thought to the obedience of Christ.
Second Corinthians 10:5

Pray that the Holy Spirit will protect your mind by showing you things to stay away from in your soul (mind), spirit, and body. Obedience to the Word and to the Holy Spirit is so very important.

Quench not the Spirit.
First Thessalonians 5:19

How do you quench the Spirit? One way is by disobeying Him.

The blood of Jesus Christ is more than enough to cleanse us from all unrighteousness. Do I believe that when you accept Jesus Christ as your Lord and Savior, His blood cleanses you from all unrighteousness, and breaks all generational curses off of you because you've become part of God's family, you are now in God's blood line, and you are the righteousness of God in Christ Jesus? Yes, absolutely! So why would it be necessary to provide any steps for deliverance as I will provide in the following pages? Because many people don't live in all of their inheritance in Christ Jesus. Many are strangers to the covenant promises and do not walk in holiness (which is obedience to God and coming into agreement with His Word). They still let the devil bring their old sins back on them.

It's for the very purpose of helping people find their deliverance that this book has been written. You *can* receive your "birth day" gifts in the form of blessings!

CHAPTER TEN

STEPS TO DELIVERANCE

1. Name all your forefathers that you can think of (parents, grandparents, and great-grandparents) if you know who they are. Then list all of their sins and all of their iniquities that you know about. Ask the Holy Spirit to show you ones you don't know.

2. Confess each individual sin. Say to God, "I have committed the sin of _____," and ask God to forgive that sin as if it was one of your own iniquities. Renounce any connection with any false religion and with the occult.

3. Renounce all self-imposed curses, (e.g., "I'm so dumb" or "I'm so fat").

4. Name your own iniquities. Confess and ask for forgiveness for each. Accept the blood sacrifice

of the Lord Jesus Christ for your iniquities and for the iniquities of your forefathers.

5. Use the authority given unto you in the name of Jesus, and break those curses on you by the blood of Jesus in the name of Jesus.

6. Declare that any curse that is upon you is broken now and broken for generations to come. Declare: *"Christ hath redeemed from the curse of the law"* (Galatians 3:13). *" Therefore if any man be in Christ, he is a new creature: old things are passed away; behold, all things are become new"* (Second Corinthians 5:17).

7. Speak blessings over yourself, over your children, and over your grandchildren. Speak the Word. Use the following scriptures (which are written out for you after step 8). Speak Psalms 91, 23, and 103:1-6; Isaiah 54:13-14,17; Ephesians 1:17-20, 3:14-20; Philippians 1:9-11, 3:8-11; Colossians 1:9-12. Proclaim those verses that claim victory over the curse that you are dealing with, such as *"By His stripes I am healed"* (see Isaiah 53:5 and First Peter 2:24) for sickness and *"God has not given me a spirit of fear, but of power, love, and a sound mind"* (see Second Timothy 1:7) for fear.

8. *"Submit yourselves therefore to God. Resist the devil, and he will flee from you"* (James 4:7). Release the power of God in and for every situation by the blood of the Lamb and the word of your testimony (see Revelation 12:11). Forgive yourself and others (if, for instance, you were abused), and trust the Lord to bring to you the healing of the related emotions.

> *This book of the law shall not depart out of thy mouth; but thou shalt meditate therein day and night, that thou mayest observe to do according to all that is written therein: for then thou shalt make thy way prosperous, and then thou shalt have good success.*
>
> Joshua 1:8

We should meditate on the scriptures and speak them forth. Scripture references from step 7 are as follows:

> *He that dwelleth in the secret place of the most High shall abide under the shadow of the Almighty. I will say of the LORD, He is my refuge and my fortress: my God; in him will I trust. Surely he shall deliver thee from the snare of the fowler, and from the noisome pestilence. He shall cover thee with his feathers,*

and under his wings shalt thou trust: his truth shall be thy shield and buckler. Thou shalt not be afraid for the terror by night; nor for the arrow that flieth by day; nor for the pestilence that walketh in darkness; nor for the destruction that wasteth at noonday. A thousand shall fall at thy side, and ten thousand at thy right hand; but it shall not come nigh thee. Only with thine eyes shalt thou behold and see the reward of the wicked. Because thou hast made the LORD, which is my refuge, even the most High, thy habitation; there shall no evil befall thee, neither shall any plague come nigh thy dwelling. For he shall give his angels charge over thee, to keep thee in all thy ways. They shall bear thee up in their hands, lest thou dash thy foot against a stone. Thou shalt tread upon the lion and adder: the young lion and the dragon shalt thou trample under feet. Because he hath set his love upon me, therefore will I deliver him: I will set him on high, because he hath known my name. He shall call upon me, and I will answer him: I will be with him in trouble; I will deliver him, and honour him. With long life will I satisfy him, and shew him my salvation. Psalm 91

The LORD is my shepherd; I shall not want. He maketh me to lie down in green pastures: he leadeth me beside the still waters. He restoreth my soul: he leadeth me in the paths of righteousness for his name's sake. Yea, though I walk through the valley of the shadow of death, I will fear no evil: for thou art with me; thy rod and thy staff they comfort me. Thou preparest a table before me in the presence of mine enemies: thou anointest my head with oil; my cup runneth over. Surely goodness and mercy shall follow me all the days of my life: and I will dwell in the house of the LORD for ever.   Psalm 23

Bless the LORD, O my soul: and all that is within me, bless his holy name. Bless the LORD, O my soul, and forget not all his benefits: Who forgiveth all thine iniquities; who healeth all thy diseases; who redeemeth thy life from destruction; who crowneth thee with lovingkindness and tender mercies; who satisfieth thy mouth with good things; so that thy youth is renewed like the eagle's. The LORD executeth righteousness and judgment for all that are oppressed.   Psalm 103:1-6

And all thy children shall be taught of the LORD; and great shall be the peace of thy children. In righteousness shalt thou be estab-

119

lished: thou shalt be far from oppression; for thou shalt not fear: and from terror; for it shall not come near thee.

No weapon that is formed against thee shall prosper; and every tongue that shall rise against thee in judgment thou shalt condemn. This is the heritage of the servants of the LORD, and their righteousness is of me, saith the LORD.   Isaiah 54:13-14,17

That the God of our Lord Jesus Christ, the Father of glory, may give unto you the spirit of wisdom and revelation in the knowledge of him: the eyes of your understanding being enlightened; that ye may know what is the hope of his calling, and what the riches of the glory of his inheritance in the saints, and what is the exceeding greatness of his power to us-ward who believe, according to the working of his mighty power, which he wrought in Christ, when he raised him from the dead, and set him at his own right hand in the heavenly places.   Ephesians 1:17-20

For this cause I bow my knees unto the Father of our Lord Jesus Christ, of whom the whole family in heaven and earth is named, that he would grant you, according to the riches of his glory, to be strengthened with might by his Spirit in the inner man; that Christ may dwell in your hearts by faith; that ye, being rooted and grounded in love, may be able to comprehend with all saints what is the breadth, and length, and depth, and height; and to know the love of Christ, which passeth knowledge, that ye might be filled with all the fulness of God. Now unto him that is able to do exceeding abundantly above all that we ask or think, according to the power that worketh in us. Ephesians 3:14-20

And this I pray, that your love may abound yet more and more in knowledge and in all judgment; that ye may approve things that are excellent; that ye may be sincere and without offence till the day of Christ; being filled with the fruits of righteousness, which are by Jesus Christ, unto the glory and praise of God. Philippians 1:9-11

Yea doubtless, and I count all things but loss for the excellency of the knowledge of Christ Jesus my Lord: for whom I have suffered the loss of all things, and do count them but dung, that I may win Christ, and be found in him, not having mine own righteous-

ness, which is of the law, but that which is through the faith of Christ, the righteousness which is of God by faith: that I may know him, and the power of his resurrection, and the fellowship of his sufferings, being made conformable unto his death; if by any means I might attain unto the resurrection of the dead. Philippians 3:8-11

For this cause we also, since the day we heard it, do not cease to pray for you, and to desire that ye might be filled with the knowledge of his will in all wisdom and spiritual understanding; that ye might walk worthy of the Lord unto all pleasing, being fruitful in every good work, and increasing in the knowledge of God; strengthened with all might, according to his glorious power, unto all patience and longsuffering with joyfulness; giving thanks unto the Father, which hath made us meet to be partakers of the inheritance of the saints in light. Colossians 1:9-12

PRAYER

Father God, I thank You that Jesus Christ has provided everything we need for deliverance from sin, from iniquities, and from curses. I declare these sins and iniquities, (name them here, e.g., grief, lying), and I repent of them.

I accept the divine sacrifice of Jesus. I know His blood was shed for my ancestors and for me, and I accept His supreme sacrifice. His blood was more than enough.

Thank You for Your blood, Your Word, Your grace, and Your Holy Spirit who is the anointing. The anointing destroys the yoke.

In Jesus name, I declare that Satan is defeated and the curse of (name the curse, e.g., lying) is broken and destroyed by the blood of Jesus and by the completed work of Christ on the cross. Satan has no place in my life or in the lives of my children, my grandchildren, or in the lives of those generations to come. Father, I now declare that I am free from the curse, and I'll walk in the blessing!

I pray in the mighty Name of Jesus. Amen.

NAMES OF GOD

God's names are listed here. There are many more. He wants to be what these names mean to you when you accept what Christ Jesus, the Anointed One, did for you. We are reconciled to God by the divine sacrifice of Jesus, through His death, burial, and resurrection.

Here are some of the names:

God is Omnipotent — All Powerful (Genesis 18:14, Deuteronomy 3:24)

God is Omnipresent — Everywhere Present, Infinitely Present (Jeremiah 23:23,24)

God is Omniscient — All Knowing (Psalm 33:13-15)

Jehovah-Rophe — The God That Heals (Exodus 15:26)

Jehovah-Nissi — Banner, Sail in the Desert (Exodus 17:8-15)

Jehovah-Shalom — Our Peace (Judges 6: 23-24)

Jehovah-Rohi — Our Shepherd — we shall not want (Psalm 23)

Jehovah-Tsidkenu — Our Righteousness (Jeremiah 33:6-8)

Jehovah-Jirah — Our Provider (Genesis 22:13-14)

Jehovah-Shammah —The Lord Is Present (Ezekiel 48:35)

El Elyon — The Most High God (Genesis 14:18-20)

El Shaddai — The All-Sufficient One (Exodus 6:3, 17: 1-6)

El Olam — The Everlasting One (Genesis 21:33)

Adonai — Our Lord and Master (Acts 2:36)

I AM THAT I AM — Whatever You May Need Is Exactly What I Am. (Exodus 3:14)

Psalm 91:14 says, *"Because he hath known my name … I will answer him: I will be with him … I will deliver him, and honour him."*

Support Keys to Ongoing Freedom

Support your freedom by fellowshipping with other believers. (Hebrews 10:25)

Support your freedom with daily prayer. (First Thessalonians 5:17)

Support your freedom with daily studying God's Word. (Second Timothy 2:15)

Support your freedom by taking every thought captive. (Second Corinthians 10:5)

Support your freedom by giving no place to the devil. (Ephesians 4:27) (James 4:7)

Support your freedom by sharing your faith. (Revelation 12:11)

The choices you make will affect your children's and grandchildren's lives for eternity. I pray you make the right ones. Make choices that are in agreement with the Word of God.